6.22. 2 0 0

For Car[...]
I love [...]
especially Powell's.
    Hope some of these
"songs" make you
        happy.
    All the best,
        Charli[e] Brice

ALL THE SONGS SUNG

CHARLIE BRICE

ANGELS FLIGHT BOOKS

ANGELS FLIGHT BOOKS

Copyright © 2021 Charlie Brice

ISBN: 978-1-7337848-2-5

Director: Kareem Tayyar
Book Design and Layout: Casandra Hernández Ríos

www.angelsflightbooks.com

For Judy

ACKNOWLEDGMENTS

Adirondack Review: "The H Word"

BOMBFIRE: "The Onion Theory of the Universe"

Flair Journal: "Journey to the Mailbox on Beech St"

Impspired Magazine (UK): "Ars Poetica III," "Garden Scene with a Watering Can"

Nine Muses Poetry: "On Our Forty-Sixth"

Uppagus: "Smoke"

The Banyan Review: "Quotidien Medley"

CONTENTS

We were alone and I was singing this song for you.
Leon Russell

Daily Mirepoix

To me, 8 AM is the middle
        of the night.
I'm an old retired guy
        who rarely rises
before 10 AM
        and then only
to recline on routine's bed:

Feed the birds, then Mugsi
        the dog, then myself—
a fresh pot of Russian tea,
        two slices of dark rye bread,
half a grapefruit, all imbibed
        with gratitude
on our back porch,

The *Times*, a service berry bush,
        violet monk's hood, chickadees,
finches (purple and gold),
        and a fallcrisp breeze
for company. There's no drama,
        no dearth or death, just life, breath—
the going-on-being of my blessed
        insignificance in this world.

Journey to the Mailbox on Beech St.

Forty years on Maple Avenue and
I'm still not sure about our cross streets.
It's embarrassing.

I can dissert on why Nietzsche collapsed
his concepts of the Dionysian and Apollonian
into the single category—Apollonian—but
I simply don't pay attention to street signs.

I walk up Maple Avenue to Beech Street
and greet sycamores, their yellow/green
sheen stately and serene. A leaf falls,
and even with perfect peripheral vision,
it doesn't notice the likes of me.

And here's a dead June Bug, evidently
what happens to June Bugs in August,
or maybe it's an August Bug who's met
a tragic early death, this being only the 24th.

All along this walk I'm guilty.
Our sweet poodle-dog, Mugsi,
wanted to accompany me and doesn't
understand why I failed to strap
on her harness and lead her out the door.

I tell myself that I'm protecting her
from the blanket of heat and humidity
that covers me on my way out,
but then a breeze across my face and arms
performs an anti-absolution of my sin.

When I turn up Beech Street, cedar-scent
wafts me toward my goal: to mail
a get-well card to my physician who
has broken his ankle, and when I squeeze
the oversized envelope into the mail slot,
I pledge to give Mugsi a mushy Nudgie treat
to compensate for this self-indulgent solo walk
on a hot and humid August day in Pittsburgh.

The H Word

We're not supposed
to write about it anymore.
It's become hackneyed, clichéd,
maudlin, saccharine, and sentimental.

Only 400 years ago, in 1653, the
English physician, William Harvey
called it a pump. But for a hundred
thousand years it had been quite something else:

the locus of love in the world, a sacred place
where religious feeling hovered, a pulsating
core of care handed to another, in trust, in hope,
a chrysalis of concern that umbrella'd

a child through existence, kept
him or her warm at night,
called the doctor, medicine man,
or shaman when a little one fell ill,

and shattered forever while wiping
tiny fingerprints from a windowpane
after a small coffin gently snuggled
into Gaia's waiting arms.

Ars Poetica III

A poem leaps off
the page grabs me
by my shirt front rips
off a few buttons
smacks me straight
in the nose
blood
my blood splatters
all over my desk oozes
out of my printer
keyboard keys hopelessly
sticky and stained

This is when I know I'm alive
dead poets dance across pages
laugh and weep
speak of grief
horse hooves on cobblestones
heart monitor's beep beep beep
cars speed through the night
an ear gentle against the ground
listens for an absent god
suicidal teen's feet inch
closer to the overpass edge
a lake laps calm as

a loon's call at dawn
cancer ward stench
sweaty sighs of entwined lovers
silence loud as a stanza break
sights seen in my midnight mind
all the songs sung
in psyche's dark tunnel

go ahead give me your best shot
I'm ready for another round

Window

If you are a devout Buddhist,
if you embody his essence,
do you praise the Buddha or spit on him?

Zen Buddhists might spit because
the Buddha is within and, like the ego,
veneration impedes enlightenment.

Tibetan Buddhists would venerate the Buddha
because they venerate everything. Still,
anything can obstruct enlightenment.

Take, for example, the Bodhisattva vow
not to attain enlightenment until all sentient
beings do. A Zen friend complains

that she gets bored waiting in the checkout
line at the grocery store much less
many millennia for nirvana.

I think it is our nature to disagree.

I look out the window on this
rainy, dreary day in Pittsburgh
at the cedar tree next door—

at its tangled web of boughs,
and it's there that I find Buddha,
it's there that I bow.

Flight Plan 1965-1985

A Librium, a single-malt scotch chaser,
another scotch at the airport,
another Librium squeezed down
my dry throat, knuckles and digits
closed in a death grip on arm rests
as I personally lift the aircraft
into the menacing, murderous skies.
Every variance in engine pitch
forecasts the final, lethal plunge,
the five hundred MPH gyre
into the unribbed earth.

Flight attendants weave through
the *tube de la mort* and hand out
shooters. I pour a couple into
the plastic death chalice in
my trembling hands and throw
down another Librium. When
the ride gets bumpy and the
pilot orders flight attendants
to take their seats, I'm gobsmacked
by the certainty of the next day's
headline: PLANE PLUMMETS
IN STORM: NO SURVIVORS.

Years later, it seems, and surprised
that I hadn't succumbed to the tachycardia
propelling my heart faster than
a turbofan, I hear the serene squeal
of wheels on runway, the soothing
sound of reverse engines, and marvel
at the miracle of breath, flesh, life itself!
As relief vibrates through my body,
I thank the pilots for delivering me from
the jaws of death, try to deplane but,
drunk and drugged, I can hardly walk.
The full force of the fierce spirits have
taken effect. I'm sloshed! The first day
of wherever I've landed wasted in a
chemical haze. Still, survival is sweet.

On Our Forty-Sixth

Twenty-five years ago I said
to my sweet wife, "They'll never
improve the picture quality
on the modern television."

"Oh yes they will," Judy replied.

I watched Judy move the focus switch
and fool with the F-Stop on her Minolta
and proclaimed, "They'll never come up
with anything simpler that will take
as good a photo as that lovely camera."

"Yes they will," Judy sighed.

When we met, forty-eight years ago,
we called each other on rotary phones.
We waited after dialing each number
for the metal dial assembly to return
to its origins before we could dial
the next number. "Won't they ever
invent a better way to make a call?"
I complained.

"They will," Judy rejoined.

And as we exchanged vows on top
of a mountain in Gold Hill, Colorado,
forty-six years ago, I said, "We'll
never love each other more than
we do today."

"Oh yes we will," Judy smiled.

And on this day, the day of our
forty-sixth wedding anniversary,
I've never been so happy about
being so wrong for so long.

M.Y.W.I.F.E.

Suitcases shifted wildly
from one side of the bus
to another. Ari and I
grabbed what we could
while we held onto the bus's
crossbars and strap-poles as if
riding a rollercoaster gone insane
on cocaine or methamphetamine.

The bus driver in Calais forgot
that he was a bus driver, instead
he'd incarnated Sterling Moss
racing down gnarled streets
of Monaco, mocking gravity
at every turn.

And what of all those bags?
I had two, Ari one, and
someone with the initials
M.Y.W.I.F.E had brought along,
on this, our first foray as a family
to France, seven large travel bags
that Ari and I had to chase while
they slid up and down the bus aisle

like hyperactive children
on sugar highs—seven bags
of "absolutely essential" stuff that
made my son and I commemorate
the martyrdom of St. Joan of Arc
on that smokey day in May, 1431.

A Rising Starr

His manner was strange,
like a nowhere man.
He wanted me to teach him
how to play the drums.
Please, please me, he pleaded.
See what I mean?

I sat him down before my brand new
Ludwig Oyster Pearl drum set
with shiny Zildjian cymbals.
Put your foot on that Speed King,
I said. Pump the bass drum pedal
to keep the beat:
one, two, three, four,
one, two, three, four.

That's it, now whack that snare
on two and four:
one, TWO, three, FOUR
one, TWO, three, FOUR.
You got it! Now
eighth notes on the ride cymbal:
one & two & three & four &
one & two & three & four &.

Feelin' it? Okay, put it all together:
one & TWO & three & FOUR &
one & TWO & three & FOUR &
You doing it, brother, I said.
Gear, he said. Fab, he said,
and kept playing this kick-beat
till he owned it.

Practice at least an hour a day,
I told him. He rolled his eyes,
but said Ta which I think meant thanks.
I handed him a pair of drumsticks.
Here, I said, take these Ludwig 3As.
Ta he said in his low Liverpool drawl.

I didn't think he'd go far.
He wore too many rings on his fingers.
When he played, they had to hurt.

The Onion Theory of the Universe

He sat across from me
at a table on the Psych Ward
at Denver General Hospital, 1970.

He cut an onion in half
with the knife I let him use
when the nurses weren't watching.

He handed me the two halves
and sat back with a wizened wink.
"See what I mean?" he said.

George taught me to play chess
seriously, to think about checkmate
from the first move onward.

He was a grizzled fellow who had,
behind the psychosis, a grandfatherly
gentleness—a flannel flair.

We had to restrict his use
of the Ward's payphone. The FBI
complained that George
kept calling to report the many

Soviet agents among his fellow
patients and our staff. His
code name, he told the Feds,
was Sargent Friday. His was

The Onion Theory of the Universe,
it's truth so apparent to him that
"see what I mean?" was his sole
and sufficient explanation.

And perhaps, if you patiently unwound
all those scale layers, you'd discover
what George did at its (and his) core.

The Secret Service had alerted
the Denver Police after George sent
over a dozen Spanish onion halves
(his favorite) to President Nixon.

Apparently, Nixon never understood
George's handwritten note, never
grasped its truth. See what I mean?

Smoke

Blue smoke rose out of the Vatican chimney
then fireworks—big color-filled splashes
in the sky. People crossed themselves.

The clang of crucifixes against worn beads
on rosaries pulled in panic from pockets was
so loud that nuns donned earmuffs in July.

A pilgrim, convinced that his self-induced
nocturnal emissions had caused this vaporous
aberration, destroyed both patellae

on his penitent crawl across the sacred
span of St. Peter's Square. The Faithful
were flummoxed! After the Pole,

the German, and the dangerous Argentinian,
they'd prayed for a return to calm, for the
ascension of a simple man with a name like

Giovani, Paulo, Amedio, or Giuseppe, but
now they quivered wide-eyed with terror as
rockets soared. Clearly a *mysterium tremendum.*

What rough beast did these pyrotechnics
portend? What prophecy propelled them?
How vicious the new Vicar's voice?

The Silent Sound of Empathy

What happens to our words
when they leave our mouths?
Whose ears do they penetrate?
What part of the brain
gives them a home?

Do they become wraiths
who wander through space,
or are they turned from outer into
inner sound—*esprit jolie?*

What is sound? Vibrations
of what is no more?
Can there be meaning
without sound? Don't we who care

love the lilt of Plato's voice?
Even an equation hums along:
What you can do to one side,
you can do to the other side—
the tonal fairness of that!

Then there's the silent
sound of empathy. I visited

for a year with a woman
whose seventeen-year-old son
had died from lupus. His throat
was sore, she thought he had a cold.
He was dead in a week. She spoke

with a fury of words. I listened silently,
at times asked her to tell me more, took
only minutes of our time while she spoke
for hours through calamitous waterfalls.
In that year of tears she paused her litany
only once, forced a smile, and said,
"You really know how to talk to me."

The Daddy of 'Em All[1]

My mother couldn't understand why
we were taking her to Pittsburgh
with us after we sprung her from
the psych ward at Memorial Hospital.

She'd been wandering around
The American National Bank
in Cheyenne looking for her CDs
and talking about death, or so said
the president of the bank who was,
in his small-town way, kind enough
to call my office in Pittsburgh.

I listened to his western twang crackle
over my answering machine: "She
could kill someone," he said, "driving
her Cadillac around town," a town
she'd lived in for fifty years,
but no longer recognized. "You'd
better come and get her, Charles."

In my mental soundtrack
I heard the guitar lick at the
beginning of "The End"

by The Doors. Certainly death
is the daddy of all ends but,
as I had just learned, death
has some powerful siblings.

[1]Traditional slogan for the Cheyenne Frontier Days rodeo

What a Piece of Work Is a Man

She liked to watch our band practice
in my basement. She liked me,
I could tell. She was thrilled
when I asked her out for a movie
at the drive-in. She was fifteen,
I was sixteen.

The bloods in our band boasted
that if the girl didn't want to put out,
they'd drive her home. Most often
she'd relent on the way and
they'd get some action.

There was also Floyd, my parents'
old friend from Portland—my father's age,
if he'd lived—who told me straight out,
in our living room, while my mother was busy
mixing drinks in the kitchen, "If they didn't
want to fuck, we just took them home."
Floyd, unlike my parents, had gone to college,
had been a fraternity man. Surely, he knew
his way around the girls.

At the drive-in, after pop and popcorn,

we settled in, my tongue in her mouth,
her body pressed tight against mine,
our breathing heavy enough to fog my car
windows in the frosty Cheyenne chill.
My hand slipped to her breast.
She moved away. It happened again.
"What?" I said.
"I don't want to do that," she said.

I stopped. I wasn't a complete asshole.
But I did what I'd learned from the bloods
and Floyd. I drove her home in silence,
parked in front of her house, and waited.
"Aren't you even going to walk me
to the door?" She asked.
"No," I said.
She got out of the car.

For a couple minutes I felt like a stud, suave,
like James Bond. Then the emptiness arrived—
that feeling when you hit an air-pocket
in a jet, plummet a few hundred feet,
hope that you'll survive.

Quotidian Medley

Life puts us in the places we need to grow.
Rosemerry Wahtola Trommer

dishwasher sough
clothes washer swish
food processor growl
bacon skillet-sizzle
burger fry-pan crackle
refrigerator hum
clothes dryer spin
vacuum cleaner howl

regenerative symphonies
soothing medleys
routine concertos
prayerful hymns

we are still here
still here
still here
still here

In My Inscape

He walks up the stairs at St. Mary's High—
"Well hi," he says in his sexy voice
to Maryanne whom he's asked to prom.

He grunts and smashes his helmet into
the big beefy guys on the other team
and wins a football scholarship to the
Colorado School of Mines.

He's in my apartment in Denver,
1970. He has refused induction
into the army, dodged the draft,
goes home to Cheyenne, waits
for federal marshalls to arrive.

He lives in the mountains near
Colorado Springs. I lose contact
with him for thirty years, but find
him again on Facebook.

He has gone through four wives
and lives by himself with
two beloved dogs.

On his 65th birthday I write, "Hey,
Visc, happy birthday old man.
Hope you have many, many more."
Someone replies to my post that
Visc had died a month earlier.

They found him dressed but shoeless
on the edge of his bed. When his father
hadn't heard from him for two weeks, he
called the sheriff. I try not to think
about how his dogs survived.

Phil

For months I searched the internet
for my old friend Phil. He'd written a book
about a trek he'd taken through the Himalayas:
memoired the massive beauty of those mountains,
the periodic intransigence of his Tibetan guides,
and how temperamental a yak could become.
At one point, a yak fell into a crevasse,
broke a leg. They had to leave him
on that snow-blistered mountain.

Phil and I objected to killing people. Assigned
to work at Denver General Hospital as hospital
attendants, post nominal letters "H.A." were placed
on our name tags. Because Phil already had a B.A.,
he wanted his nametag to read, *Phil Druker*, B.A. H.A
(BA HA BA HA BA HAHAHA!).

One night, as we prepared to pass food trays
to our patients on the Psych Ward, a distracted
Phil drove the food cart over my foot. I hated him
while my ankle throbbed. In the ER, a sleepy intern
wrapped my foot in a bandage. Jolted awake at 3AM
by pulsating pain, I tore the bandage from my foot
and hated the careless, callow, intern who'd

wrapped my foot too tightly.

Forty years later, my trek through the internet
succeeded. I called Phil. His speech slurred
from morphine-sated terminal cancer. We
talked about bedpans and patients who bit,
about his book, Buddhism, and meditation. Had
it helped with the pain? Not really, he sighed.
Finally, we had to say goodbye. "Thanks
for finding me," he said. "I'll never forget it."
Two days after our call, he died.

Phil died today, I wrote at the top of the page
I was reading and put his book back on my shelf
where it sits today like a yak,
frozen and waiting.

What If You Slept

After "What if You Slept" by Samuel Taylor Coleridge

and your mother was smiling and kind,
reading books, sampling strawberries,
her favorite fruit, and packing picnics—
what she always wanted to do
had it not been for Budweiser
and your father; and your father
was singing as he did in the mornings:
"Thanks for the Memories,"
and "Blue Skies" and was sober
and fighting trim; and you were
playing catch with your son
when he was eight, kick ball
when he was ten, watching him
zig-zag down a double black diamond
at seventeen, holding his carefully
crafted cups and bowls in his twenties,
watching the Pirates play the Dodgers
together in his forties; and Judy's
long midnight hair hangs
on her shoulders and her doe-eyes
glitter in their seductive and
irresistible ways and she takes

your hand and you dance with her
atop her lilting verses and stars
explode, planets spiral through space
vaporizing vapors, dissolving black holes,
revising your time on this earthly cyst
into an eternal remonstration of redemption,
wrapping you in a celestial blanket of bliss,
and you hear the English horn's calm
call that belongs to Dvorak's largo theme,
and you stand, hands outstretched to life,
and it's then that you understand
that you died while you slept?

Garden Scene with a Watering Can

After the painting by Paul Klee

The garden blooms in peaceful excitement.
Watering cans, shy, diffident, reside
ready for their quenching duty.

An empty sky-blue work bucket,
its handle resting in repose, announces
the day's work complete, waits

to catch the cat's contented purr
purl from its perch atop
a patio table next to a lounge chair

we want to inhabit—we who,
with hand shovel and hoe, grow
art in our backyards, slip off

work gloves amid earthen smells
and trembling leaves, put-up our feet
and dream a wild palette of color.

Breakfast

Pour water into the kettle,
put it on the burner,
clean the litter box,
give the cats water,
feed the dog, recite
Roethke's "My Papa's Waltz."
Scald out the teapot, place
one teaspoon of tea for the pot,
another for yourself,
savor the soothing sound
of the teakettle's whistle,
pour water into the pot for tea.
Put an egg in a pan of water,
place it on the burner, recite
Jim Harrison's poem, "Counting Birds,"
wait for the egg-water to boil,
set the timer for three minutes.
Grab a slice of bread,
put it in the toaster, recite
"When You are Old and Gray," by Yeats.
Slice a grapefruit in half,
ream out the succulent sections
with a serrated knife, celebrate
the fragrance of fresh citrus.

Secure a small plate for the toast and egg,
a knife and a fork,
stir the tea, heat the milk, and recite
"Spring and Fall," by Gerard Manly Hopkins.
When the timer chimes
pour out the boiling water
and trickle in some cold,
not enough to crack the egg,
but enough so you can hold it.
Plate the toast and decapitate the egg.
Scoop the yoke and the white
onto the toast. Don't let the yoke
run over the toast onto the plate.
Pour milk and tea into the mug you won
in a poetry contest years back.
Eat and drink everything while it's
hot and juicy. Smile and recite
Tom Lux's, "Poem in Thanks."

Charlie Brice is a retired psychoanalyst and is the author of *Flashcuts Out of Chaos* (WordTech Editions, 2016) and *Mnemosyne's Hand* (WordTech Editions, 2018). His poetry has been nominated for the Best of the Net anthology and a Pushcart Prize and has appeared in *The Atlanta Review*, *Hawaii Review*, *The Main Street Rag*, *Chiron Review*, *Fifth Wednesday Journal*, *SLAB*, *The Paterson Literary Review*, *Muddy River Poetry Review* and elsewhere.

CPSIA information can be obtained
at www.ICGtesting.com
Printed in the USA
BVHW070246150421
604862BV00001B/46